STRESS TO *calm* IN 7 MINUTES

FOR LAWYERS

BEVERLEY DENSHAM
& JANEY LEE GRACE

McNIDDER & GRACE

Published by McNidder & Grace
21 Bridge Street
Carmarthen
SA31 3JS
Wales, UK

www.mcnidderandgrace.com

First published in 2024

A catalogue record for this work is available from the British Library.

ISBN 9780857162526 paperback
ISBN 9780857162533 ebook

Designer: JS Typesetting
Cover design: Tabitha Palmer

FOREWORD

Frazzled, lacking sleep, struggling, and feeling stressed? Then this book is for you.

I am a solicitor in my 50s, and I am busy. I love my work, but it is demanding. My body and my mind are not as resilient as they once were. Menopause, age, the pressure of working and running my own business have taken their toll. I was aware that I needed to make lifestyle changes but not sure where to start.

I started working with Bev to help manage my back pain and stress using a programme she devised to teach lawyers how to manage stress and counteract the effects of long hours spent at a desk.

I began to understand that *finding time* to *consistently* practice self-care was important to my health and well-being and just finding that spare 7 minutes per day was enough to make the difference.

Working the 7-minute programme has been a revelation. I am amazed by what can be achieved in such a short amount of time. The combination of techniques; breathing, meditation, visualisation, stretches, journaling, relaxation, positive affirmations, and goal setting is great. The techniques are easy to follow, and their effect is immediate.

My favourite is the breathing which has changed my life, but I also love stretching, journaling and the happy exercise which just makes me smile every single time.

I am proud to have been asked to write this Foreword and proud to have changed my life for the better by following its teaching. I know your experience will be as positive and as life changing as it has been for me both professionally and personally.

Anna Illingworth, 2023
Partner, Rowberry Morris Solicitors

CONTENTS

INTRODUCTION
STRESS TO CALM ...

If you've picked up this book, we're guessing it's because a part of you knows that your current stress levels are not sustainable. Something has to give!

Let us start by giving you hope that after reading this book, you will have some very simple tools that will help you to feel more in control and calmer.

When emotions start to run out of control, we will teach you to say – **just give me one minute!** And we will show you the one-minute tools that will make you feel so much better, and quickly.

For many of us, stress has become an inevitable part of our lives. From managing work deadlines to balancing personal commitments, we can easily become overwhelmed and consumed by stress. And for lawyers, this stress can be compounded by the high-stakes and often high-pressure nature of their work.

Stress is often viewed as a negative experience that should be avoided or minimised at all costs. But it's a common myth that stress is always bad for us. Stress is a natural response to challenging situations and can be helpful in certain circumstances. In fact, the release of cortisol, a stress hormone, is a necessary physiological reaction that allows us to react quickly in dangerous or stressful situations, such as the 'fight or flight' response. Where it goes wrong, is when we perceive our bulging file of work to take home as a predator about to attack!

When we encounter a stressful situation, our body releases cortisol, adrenaline and other hormones that trigger a series of physical responses. These responses include an increase in heart rate, blood pressure and breathing rate, which prepares the body to respond quickly to the threat. This physiological response is useful when there is a real physical threat, such as being chased by a tiger. Our ancestors needed that ability to focus on their escape ... and fast! Sadly, we have the same response in our modern world. But in the office, in the courtroom, surrounded by colleagues and a legal team, even when back home – there are no tigers!

The heart can be pounding, the 'threat' feels very real, but this full stress response is inappropriate. What we are confronting may genuinely be a big problem – concerns about a deadline or an outcome for a client in the courtroom – and there may seemingly be no positive solutions, but it isn't life-threatening, it isn't a real and present danger, and so these physical responses can have negative consequences on our wellbeing. We aren't meant to constantly release these chemicals, and the prolonged exposure to cortisol and other stress hormones can lead to physical and emotional health problems over time, including anxiety, depression, high blood pressure and a weakened immune system. It can lead to burnout and fatigue, making it difficult to function effectively in our daily lives. In addition to the physical impact, when our minds are consumed with panic, destructive thoughts and incessant chatter, we can fall into patterns of negative thinking which can impact our mental health and overall outlook on life.

We presume that as a lawyer or a professional in a legal capacity you are in control in your professional life. If you do not currently feel this to be the case, we want you to feel empowered and in control in your professional capacity – and these simple tools we share with you in this book will help you find more of a sense of calm and balance. They will help you manage the stresses in your working day. These tools are practical and based on scientifically proven methods that will reduce stress, empower you to take control of your stress levels and improve your overall wellbeing.

The tools in this book are designed to be easily incorporated into a busy lawyer's daily routine. They can be done in just a few minutes a day and they require no special equipment or training. We will explore techniques such as breathing exercises, mindfulness, positive affirmations and visualisation, all of which have been shown to reduce stress and promote calm.

We will explore the concept of choosing happiness. Yes, we show you that this can be a choice! We look at the importance of setting goals for both work and personal life. We also learn to focus on positive outcomes and how to take small steps towards achieving them, to shift your mindset and cultivating a more positive outlook.

Throughout the book, we will cite scientific studies that demonstrate the benefits of each technique we discuss. For example, studies have shown that mindfulness can reduce stress and anxiety levels, while breathing exercises can lower cortisol levels and improve heart health. We hope you will be able to utilise the real and tangible benefits of these simple tools and techniques.

The legal profession can be highly demanding, but that doesn't mean lawyers have to sacrifice their wellbeing in the process. By incorporating the tools presented in this book, lawyers can take control of their stress levels and achieve a greater sense of balance and calm. We hope this book serves as a valuable resource and inspires you to take small but meaningful steps towards a happier and healthier life.

So why *are* lawyers feeling the need to go from Stress to Calm?

What are the main problems that lawyers face – and why is this profession prone to stress? We asked some lawyers in an independent survey and their responses were quite revealing. We have changed all names to protect their identity.

Deidre has been a solicitor for 20 years and a corporate law partner in a law firm for about 8 years. She describes her severe stress being exacerbated by deadlines caused by clients who *'need matters completed within a certain deadline, coupled with the concern that you have given clients the correct advice / not missed anything which might result in a legal issue later.'*

Deirdre says: *'Often lots of work comes along at once and all clients want to take priority! We are a service profession, so in theory the client comes first – and if that means working late or at weekends or early mornings, you must do it. I think all solicitors worry to a greater or lesser extent that they have kept their clients happy.'*

Deirdre also feels that her work stress impacts on her home and personal life.

'If I am very *stressed about a specific work issue, I tend to wake at 4 a.m. and then worry over specific client issues which, in the light of day, are not big problems. My job is very sedentary and while I walk to and from work and try to exercise every day, if things are busy, I will often be in work from around 7.30/8 a.m. to 8/9 p.m. and not have time to exercise as I feel too exhausted. I am very bad with food. I am overweight and often cannot be bothered to cook and will just grab something on the way home or call for a home delivery takeaway!'*

Stacey has been a lawyer for 16 years. She worries about managing conflicting client priorities and internal needs. For example, team management causes a lot of stress, and she also explains that she feels the *'consequences of getting something wrong'* to be a significant cause of stress.

Stacey says: *'My practice is transaction based, so when matters approach completion the hours can be very long and the pressure can be intense. I suspect most lawyers would say the same thing! But pressures can be different for different types of law – for example, in my team we don't have to deal with court deadlines.*

Stacey also says she can't find enough time to exercise, and work-related stress does impact on sleep. *'I try to switch off, but working from home part of the time does blur that line between the spheres of life and requires discipline to turn the laptop off until the morning. I'm careful about diet as I definitely think the better we eat, the better we feel, so as a family we do eat pretty healthy a lot of the time.'*

Jacqui is a family solicitor. She agrees stress often comes from pressure from clients to meet certain deadlines or from addressing the gap between their expectations and the legal reality/likely outcome. Jacqui also reiterates that having a number of cases which all need attention at the same time can cause stress.

Sunita is a human rights lawyer:

'Stress is pervasive in our sector given the nature of the work that we do. In my area of human rights, I am confronted by very challenging issues every day. I started life as an immigration and asylum lawyer and represented people who had fled situations where they had been tortured, ill-treated and/or subjected to sexual violence. I heard those stories, and their testimony deeply affected me. The concept of "vicarious trauma" is very real for human rights lawyers/advocates

and we take on some of the trauma that our clients have suffered in their own lives. In addition, burnout is a real issue for human rights lawyers; we feel a deep need to "fix the world" in some way and we can't close the doors always. We take our work home with us and it is difficult for us to switch off at the end of the day. I think it might be a bit easier for lawyers who work in other sectors, but they probably have their own stresses and pressures. I do try and practise as much self-care as I'm able. I have six nieces and nephews and I love to spend time with them; it helps me with reducing my stress levels.'

Nerpal is an immigration lawyer and also feels overwhelmed.

'Lawyers do have large caseloads, and challenging work environments. I know that I felt overwhelmed when I practised as an immigration and asylum lawyer; I had a very large caseload and felt very stressed and worried about how I could service all my clients in a professional way. Often it just wasn't possible, and I took that distress to heart.'

Steve has been a legal adviser for over 20 years in crime as well as estate planning.

Steve says: *'The stresses are dealing with police when they are being obstructive. Custody phones go on answerphone, leaving you waiting in custody and not being updated. This impacts on other arranged times and it all has a knock-on effect.*

'I try not to bring the stress home, but at times it seeps in. It can take a good 30 minutes to adjust. My sleep is bad! My diet isn't great either, but my wife works hard keeping this in check for me.'

For some lawyers it all got too much. Samantha left the profession after working for 35 years as a family lawyer/ mediator/trainer.

She remembers the *'emotional contagion'* from highly stressed clients, and secondary anxiety about very difficult family and relationship dynamics; high-conflict litigation; Friday late afternoon emails; and stress from the broken court system.

We asked the lawyers whether any help was provided within their workplace settings and here are some of the responses:

'My company does provide wellbeing workshops and has an open-door policy with regards to anyone suffering with mental health. I have not attended any of these. I do think we would benefit from organised away days as a firm – even if it is something as simple as bowling or a picnic in a park – I may just suggest these now!'

'Nothing is offered for us, we are a really small firm of just 3, so it hasn't been a priority in terms of budget or time.'

'I'm self-employed now, but when I was an employee, all the firms I worked for provided initiatives – e.g., Pilates at lunchtime, workshops to manage time, counselling services – and it was appreciated.'

'Our staff all has access to a counselling service that they can access without us knowing. Several members of staff have used the service on several occasions. As well as stress-relieving sessions, we have briefings twice a week and help each other out and discuss workloads and stress levels.'

So, it's a mixed bag regarding workplace support, but what we hope is that the tools we describe can be incorporated into your daily life and will make a real difference.

The tools – the lowdown

We will cover some techniques in this book that you will already be aware of, and some that might be new to you. Everyone has heard of meditation (though you may not realise how to do it or that even one minute of meditation can be beneficial). You may be aware that stretching, good posture and breathing techniques can help with stress. You may have come across the Power Pose, which we can't wait to share with you, and you may be aware of the power of positive affirmations, or journaling. In any case, we will give you the lowdown on why these practices can work so well to relieve stress, and we give you very simple versions that can be done anywhere and in one minute or less!

A word about *mindfulness*, which is not one of the designated practices in this book. You may wonder why. It's become rather a catch-all term in recent years, but we would hope that you can practise mindfulness almost without trying, when you use these tools.

Mindfulness is the practice of intentionally focusing your attention on the present moment. It involves paying attention to your thoughts, feelings and bodily sensations, in a non-judgmental way. Mindfulness has been shown to be an effective way to reduce stress and anxiety and it can help you to improve your focus and concentration. We think that all the tools and techniques we share in this book could come under the banner of 'being mindful'.

How to use this book

Each short chapter gives you a stress to calm technique that should take only one minute per day. Put these seven one-minute techniques together from each of the seven chapters and you will have a set of tools that takes just seven minutes!

In an ideal world you could read each of the short chapters and then start using them straight away – ideally all seven every day – but you can of course pick out any that appeal and just give it a go, whenever suits you.

In time you can adapt these techniques and use the ones that work for you best. We appreciate that you may not want to be punching the air on the train home or adopting a power pose as you stand in front of the judge in a courtroom(!), but you can always find a moment to fit these tools into your day.

But if you are someone who likes to flick through, or even start at the back of the book **– we see you –** that's fine too.

It's as easy as saying: **Just give me one minute!** and then using that minute to try any one of these tools and then notice if repetition begins to make a difference.

We would love to know how you get on, so do send any feedback to us. You'll find our contact details are towards the end of this book.

CHAPTER ONE

STRESS TO CALM WITH MEDITATION

Tip: Remember it's just ONE minute –
you do NOT have to levitate!

What's the lowdown?

All of us have heard of meditation, and many of us have tried it – but given up when we realised that sitting for 20 minutes while our mind wandered off to write shopping lists or worry about our next work project, might not suit us. The reality is, when you find a way to meditate that works, it's liberating, and as we are going to show here, it can take as little as one minute.

Meditation is a powerful tool that can help to reduce stress, improve mental clarity and bring a sense of calm and balance to our lives. Contrary to popular belief, meditation does not have to be done in a certain way or for a certain length of time. Even a minute or so of meditation per day can be hugely beneficial for calming the mind and reducing stress.

One of the primary benefits of meditation is its ability to help us manage stress. When we are stressed, our bodies release a hormone called cortisol, which can have negative effects on our health if it is consistently elevated. However, studies have shown that regular meditation can help to reduce cortisol levels, which in turn can lead to a reduction in stress and anxiety.

Meditation can also help to improve mental clarity and focus. It helps us with mindfulness and being more present, more in the moment. We become more aware of our thoughts and emotions and learn to better manage them. This can lead to a greater sense of inner peace and clarity and can help us to approach our daily tasks with greater focus and more productivity.

'Through meditation and by giving full attention to one thing at a time, we can learn to direct attention where we choose.'

Eknath Easwaran, spiritual teacher

There are many ways to meditate, and it is important to find a method that works for you. Some people prefer to sit on a mat or a cushion, while others prefer to lie down or sit in a chair. The key is to find a comfortable position that allows you to relax and focus your mind. You absolutely can utilise your time on the train, or at your desk;

let go of the idea that it must be a long session sitting cross-legged.

One popular method of meditation is mindfulness meditation, which involves focusing on the present moment and observing your thoughts and emotions without judgment.

To practise *mindfulness meditation*, find a quiet place to sit or lie down and focus on your breath. Notice the sensations of your breath as it enters and exits your body and allow your thoughts to come and go without getting caught up in them. It's that simple!

Another method of meditation is *guided meditation*, which involves listening to a recorded meditation that guides you through the process. This can be especially helpful for beginners because it provides structure and support as you learn to quiet your mind and focus your attention.

Meditation can be incorporated into your daily routine, even if you are busy or at work. For example, you can take a few minutes to focus on your breath and observe your thoughts and emotions during a break or before a meeting. You can also try a *walking meditation*, which involves focusing on the sensations of your body as you walk and being fully present in the moment.

You will obviously have your eyes open as you walk, but meditation can be done with eyes open. This is called (not surprisingly) *open-eye meditation* or *focused attention meditation* and is a technique that involves maintaining a relaxed and focused state of mind while keeping your eyes open and fixating your gaze on an object or a point. This can be a helpful practice for those who want to integrate mindfulness into their daily routine.

You could try simply focusing on your breath while at your desk. Take a few deep breaths and then focus your attention on your breath and then continue to work. Whenever your mind starts to wander or you feel distracted, bring your attention back to your breath. This can help you reduce stress and increase productivity by bringing more focus and clarity to your work. The key is to maintain a relaxed and focused state of mind while keeping your eyes open and fixating your gaze on an object or your breath. With practice, open-eye meditation can be just as effective as traditional meditation for reducing stress and promoting overall wellbeing.

Many people have spoken about the benefits of meditation. Oprah Winfrey described meditation as a transformative practice that has helped her to manage stress and stay grounded.

Many scientific studies have demonstrated the benefits of meditation. One study published in the journal *Frontiers in Human Neuroscience* found that just four days of mindfulness meditation led to significant improvements in mood and working memory capacity. Another study, published in the *Journal of Alternative and Complementary Medicine*, found that mindfulness meditation led to significant reductions in anxiety and depression.

So, don't knock this one till you have tried it!

Meditation really is a powerful tool that can help to reduce stress, improve mental clarity and bring a sense of calm and balance to our lives. If you find your mind wandering off the first few times you try it, just relax, it's OK! Let go of the idea that we must clear our mind of all thoughts; that's unlikely to happen. What is possible, though, is that we show up anyway, consciously focus on our breath and observe the thoughts that pop up, and then we can reap the many benefits that meditation has to offer.

A word about breathing

We all breathe … of course we do, but it's enlightening when we realise that just by becoming conscious of the way we are breathing, we can almost instantly reduce our anxiety. Our breath is a reaction to our mental state:

when we are stressed, we breathe too fast, and can even hyperventilate.

We can proactively slow down our breathing. Controlling our breath will have a direct effect on us at a psychological level: it can help with hormone function, reduce inflammation, release endorphins and calm anxiety.

Simply by focusing on our breath and practising different breath work exercises, we can regulate our nervous system, slow down our heart rate, and improve our overall sense of wellbeing, we may become happier because of the naturally released neurotransmitters.

Leading breath work practitioner Tim Van de Vliet says: 'If you can control your breath, you control your life.'

By focusing on our breath and practising different techniques, we can regulate our nervous system and improve our ability to cope with stress.

TOOL 1

Let's Meditate – give me just one minute!

You can enjoy this at your desk, sitting, standing or lying down.

Before you start, check in with how you are feeling in relation to your stress levels.

You may want to select a level from 0 (feeling completely fine) to 10 (feeling very stressed). What level are you at this moment?

If you are sitting, please don't sit like a banana – i.e., bent over! Sit with good posture, with your bottom at the back of the chair, with your feet hip-width apart, and with your head, neck, shoulders and back relaxed.

If you're standing, stand with good posture – with a natural curve of your spine, with your feet hip-width apart and a slight bend in your knees. Look forwards and relax your arms down by your side.

Lie down if you have the luxury of a private space and it's comfortable for you, and if you want more back support, bend your knees, again with your feet hip-width apart.

Close your eyes, focus and concentrate on your breathing. Take 10 relaxing breaths in and out – in through your nose and out through your mouth – and relax with each breath. Feel your tummy rise and fall. Relax as you breathe in and out. Relax your head, neck and shoulders, then relax your back hips and thighs, relax your legs feet and toes, relax your arms, hands and fingers. By the end of the 10 breaths your whole body should feel releaxed.

Say 'Well done' to yourself during the breathing exercise, out loud or silently; both work well as an affirmation.

You can set an alarm for 1 minute for this meditation exercise or simply enjoy 10 relaxing breaths in and out.

Think about how you feel afterwards.

Check in to see if the stress level number you selected before you did the exercise has reduced.

CHAPTER TWO

STRESS TO CALM WITH POSITIVE AFFIRMATIONS

Tip: Remember it's just ONE minute – and you can have a CALM day!

What's the lowdown?

Positive affirmations are statements or phrases that are repeated with the intention of instilling a positive belief or attitude. The idea behind positive affirmations is that by repeating these positive statements, we can change our subconscious thought patterns, and ultimately our behaviour and emotions. Positive affirmations can work to reduce stress by helping to reframe negative thought patterns and shift our focus to positive beliefs and outcomes.

Our unconscious mind is not wired to focus on the positive, which is why many people find it difficult to introduce positive affirmations into their daily routine. The human brain tends to be wired to focus on threats and negative stimuli as a survival mechanism – we are on the lookout for danger! However, with consistent practice, positive affirmations can help to rewire the brain and promote positive thinking and emotional regulation.

Author Louise Hay wrote extensively on the power of positive affirmations. She believed that affirmations could help individuals to release negative thought patterns and improve mental and physical wellbeing. There are several scientific studies that support the effectiveness of positive affirmations for reducing stress and promoting wellbeing.

Some simple ways to introduce positive affirmations into your daily routine include writing them down, repeating them out loud, picking out a positive affirmation card, or visualising them during meditation or relaxation exercises.

You have probably heard of the idea of repeating positive affirmations/statements about yourself, to make you feel more positive. Sadly our unconscious mind has a strong bullshit detector! If we state something that feels too far-fetched for us – 'I am incredibly beautiful!' – our inner critic may tell us, 'No you're not.' So, if you tell yourself 'I am relaxed' when you are chilling at home, you may believe the affirmation, but if you're at work and feeling stressed and anxious, this affirmation probably won't work, we can't lie to ourselves! Unless, that is, you first take some action to make it feel possible. For example, you could use the meditation tool in Chapter One, which can help you change your state quickly from a stressed to a calmer state, with the result that the 'I am relaxed' affirmation will feel relevant and effective.

It might feel like too much of a stretch to declare: 'I am enthusiastic and full of energy', but you could consider what that affirmation means to you, and why it feels important.

Later in this book (see page 49), we talk about journaling, and how writing down what affirmations means to you can help. Let's take a quick peek now. For example, if you aren't feeling full of energy, you could jot down in your notebook: 'How can I find more energy? What action steps am I going to take to improve my energy levels?' We will teach you how to respond/react to these questions. Sometimes it might be as simple as getting a good night's sleep, getting to bed earlier and relaxing before you go to sleep.

We must consciously choose to repeat positive affirmations. Sadly, the negative statements often flow in our thoughts more easily, but we should be conscious of that too. When we repeatedly say: 'I am stressed', we are instructing our unconscious mind to keep us in that state of stress.

It helps to start noticing your negative thoughts and ask if there is something that could turn them around. Perhaps you just need a two-minute break to breathe and do some stretching or take a walk and get some fresh air. Or maybe you need some form of connection with others, to talk to one of your work colleagues or to seek help from a professional about what is on your mind.

Positive Affirmation cards can help. These are a set of cards with statements that help prompt you to think about something positive. If you have a set of Positive Affirmation cards, pick one out and consider what the message means to you. If you are picking a positive affirmation with a friend, family or work colleague, talk to each other about what this positive affirmation means to you, then swap over. It can lead into interesting conversations, enabling you to laugh or talk about things you need to get off your chest.

Positive affirmations help you to challenge yourself to think, speak, write and behave more positively at work and at home.

An affirmation can also be used like a mantra, to be repeated to give you more confidence in a situation outside of your comfort zone, such as needing to speak in a public situation. You might say to yourself: 'I can do this' or 'It's going to be OK.' Choose a positive statement that feels good to you.

'I can and I will. Watch me.'
Carrie Green, entrepreneur

There are several scientific studies that support the effectiveness of positive affirmations for reducing stress and promoting wellbeing. For example, a study by Moser *et al.* (2016) found that participants who practised self-affirmation exercises reported lower levels of stress and greater emotional resilience in response to a stressful task. Another study by Latham and Locke (2007) found that individuals who used positive self-talk and affirmations were more likely to achieve their goals and experience greater levels of success and wellbeing.

Practise this. Practice makes ... not exactly perfect, but it will lead to an improvement in your stress levels. Repeating the practice of using positive affirmations or using positive affirmation cards on a daily or regular basis really can make a real difference.

A study published by the US National Library of Medicine suggests that incorporating self-affirmations into a daily routine can be a powerful tool for improving mental and emotional wellbeing, reducing stress and promoting personal growth. According to the study, affirmations can reduce stress, improve wellbeing, enhance academic performance and make people more open to behaviour change. The study also recommends using positive, truthful statements as affirmations, such as 'I get on well with my child/children, mum and sister.' This kind of affirmation can be especially helpful when dealing with challenging or negative situations involving specific people or relationships.

TOOL 2

Using Positive Affirmations – give me just one minute!

Using positive affirmations can be done at the desk, at work or home, with a work colleague, friend or family or on your own.

Pick an affirmation from the list below:

I am calm, I am loved, I am surrounded by love.

I learn from my mistakes. I learn from mine and other people's mistakes.

I think positive words. When negativity appears, I find a solution, talk to those I trust and choose positivity.

It's going to be OK.

I can have fun, I am happy.

I am creative.

I enjoy exercise.

I always have lots of good ideas.

I am energetic.

I radiate positive energy wherever I go.

I am healthy.

I have good relationships.

I am strong.

I am kind.

I am grateful.

I am myself, it's OK to be myself.

I enjoy spending time with friends or family and have good relationships.

I am peaceful.

Repeat the positive affirmation you have chosen to yourself 3 times.

Think about what this means to you today.

If you don't feel what the affirmation is describing, ask yourself, *How can I feel more like this affirmation today? Are there any action steps for me to take to feel more like this affirmation to improve my life or work?*

Write down what tips and action steps you came up with.

Don't feel impatient or irritated with yourself if you can't feel like you should when repeating the affirmation. Think about how you can put steps in place in your life and work to make this feeling happen.

You can do this exercise with someone else by picking an affirmation from the list and then each of you have a turn talking about what the positive affirmation message means to you.

CHAPTER THREE

STRESS TO CALM WITH NECK AND SHOULDER STRETCHES

Tip: Remember it's just ONE minute – and you will feel GREAT after a big stretch!

What's the lowdown?

Stretching is a simple yet effective way to reduce stress, improve flexibility and alleviate back pain. It's good for emotional wellbeing too. Most of us know this or do this automatically – like doing a big stretch and a yawn when we first wake up. You will notice dogs do this intuitively and are good at stretching. In yoga there is a pose called Downward Dog! Young children naturally stretch a lot too, instinctively knowing that it's good for their body, but sadly we tend to forget as we get older or get out of the habit of doing it, especially if we are working. Instead of stretching, and sitting with good posture, we tend to tighten everything up, and then wonder why we feel like a coiled spring!

When we sit at a desk for extended periods, our muscles tend to tighten, causing discomfort and stiffness. Stretching helps to loosen these muscles, improving blood flow and oxygenation, which can help to reduce stress and anxiety. Stretching can help to improve posture too, which can reduce the likelihood of developing back pain.

In terms of physical benefits, stretching has been shown to increase flexibility, improve range of motion and reduce the risk of injury. A study published in *The Journal of Strength and Conditioning Research* found that stretching for just 30 seconds improved flexibility and range of motion in participants. Additionally, a study published in the *Clinical Journal of Sport Medicine* found that stretching reduced the risk of injury in athletes. So, remember to stretch!

'It's a good idea to always do something relaxing prior to making an important decision in your life.'
Paulo Coelho, author

Stretching can also have emotional benefits. A study published in the *International Journal of Workplace Health Management* found that stretching at work can improve mood, reduce stress and increase job satisfaction. Another study published in the *Journal of Bodywork and*

Movement Therapies found that stretching can help to reduce anxiety and depression.

Stretching well does not require a gym session and simple stretches that can be done at a desk or in a small space can be beneficial. Neck stretches, shoulder stretches, and wrist stretches can all be done at a desk. Even a minute of stretching can have benefits, and it can be done anywhere, making it an accessible and convenient self-care practice.

It's worth mentioning that being conscious of your breathing as you stretch helps too.

TOOL 3

Stretching Your Neck and Shoulders – give me just one minute!

To begin with, let's just keep it simple. Start by breathing in and out slowly and begin to follow the instructions below.

Shoulder circles

Sit or stand with good posture and with your eyes looking forward. Set an alarm for 1 minute.

Relax your arms down by your side, and circle both your shoulders 5 times backwards, lifting the shoulders up and back and round in a circular small movement. Then circle both your shoulders 5 times forward, again in small circular movements.

This will loosen your shoulders and upper body and make you feel more relaxed.

Neck stretches

• Tilt

Relax your arms down by your side. Tilt your head to the side (as if moving your ear down towards your shoulder) and feel the stretch in the side of the neck, and then tilt the head to the other side. Listen to your body, moving only as far as is comfortable for you; it's a small, slow, controlled movement. Repeat 3 times each side.

Breathe naturally, breathing in through your nose and moving on the out breath. As you exhale move and hold, then breathe in and go back to the starting position.

• Chin to chest

Relax your arms down by your side. Sitting or standing with good posture, slowly bring your chin towards your chest to gently stretch your neck to mid back muscles, then bring your head back to the starting position.

Breathe naturally, breathing in through your nose and moving on the out breath. As you exhale, move and hold, then breathe in and go back to the starting position.

• **Turn**

Relax your arms down by your side. Sitting or standing with good posture, slowly turn your head one way, then turn your head the other way. Repeat this 2–5 times.

Breathe naturally, breathing in through your nose and moving on the out breath. As you exhale, move and hold, then breathe in and go back to the starting position.

Notice how much better you feel after these simple stretches.

Bonus Tools

As you do your stretches, you can either breathe naturally or, if you want to try something a little more complex, you can focus on a style of breathing that is taught in Pilates, called 'lateral thoracic breathing'. Put your hands on your rib cage and take a deep breath through the nose, feeling the breath inside and to the back of your body. You should feel your ribs pushing your hands outward as you breathe in.

If you want to develop your breathing technique, try deep breathing. This involves taking slow, deep breaths from the diaphragm, filling your lungs with air and then exhaling slowly. Breathe into the tummy and let your tummy rise and fall as you breathe. Research has found that deep breathing can lower your stress and anxiety levels and improve your feeling of wellbeing.

You could also try the 4-7-8 breathing technique. This involves inhaling for 4 seconds, holding your breath for 7 seconds and exhaling for 8 seconds. A study published by the *Journal of Alternative and Complementary Medicine* found this technique can help reduce stress and improve sleep quality.

Next time you can't sleep, give this a try, and see if it works for you!

CHAPTER FOUR

STRESS TO CALM WITH THE POWER STRETCH

Tip: Remember it's just ONE minute – and you can FEEL the power!

What's the lowdown?

If we are feeling stressed, or a bit blue, our body tends to reflect that: everything seems to 'go downward'. We can find ourselves putting our head in our hands, slumping over and generally slipping down our chair, or hunching over if we are standing up.

It's possible to make a conscious choice to be happy, and literally change the way you feel, or change your state of mind.

We know there is a link between body and mind, and just a fearful thought can have a physiological effect on our body. Ever felt fearful and needed to run to the loo? Unconsciously our body reacts to stress in strange ways, impacting our thoughts and emotions, but we can consciously use our body to impact our thoughts and emotions in a positive way.

The mind-body connection that explores the relationship between our thoughts, emotions and physical sensations is well researched. We've heard it described as the Cybernetic Loop – the idea that the mind affects the body, but the body can affect the mind.

Let's explore this further. Have you heard of the Power Pose? It's about assuming a posture that conveys confidence, strength and assertiveness. By consciously adopting certain postures, we can positively impact our mental state and improve our sense of self-assurance.

'I am not afraid; I was born to do this.'
Joan of Arc

Research conducted by social psychologist Amy Cuddy, who gave a very popular TED Talk called 'Your body language may shape who you are', explored the effects of power poses on an individual's feelings of power, confidence and performance. Studies indicated that adopting high-power poses such as standing tall with an open posture and outstretched arms for a brief period can lead to increased feelings of power and reduced stress levels.

By adopting a power pose, we can alter hormone levels, increase testosterone (associated with dominance and confidence) and decrease cortisol (a stress hormone). These hormonal changes may contribute to the reported psychological effects.

The jury is out as to what extent we will increase testosterone just by standing up! But the broader concept of the mind-body connection is well-established. Our physical state can influence our mental state, and vice versa.

How does posture impact on our happiness?

The concept of choosing happiness involves recognising happiness as a choice that we can make in any moment, regardless of external circumstances. (More on this in Chapter Five.)

By changing our thoughts and focusing on positive emotions, we can move from feeling stressed to feeling calm in a very short space of time. Posture can also play a role in this process, as adopting a more upright and confident posture can help to improve mood and reduce stress.

Studies have shown that choosing happiness and changing our state can have a range of benefits. One study published in the journal *Emotion* found that adopting a more upright and open body posture can increase feelings of power and confidence, leading to more positive emotions.

By taking back control over our unconscious mind and changing our body posture to feel happier, we can improve our wellbeing and reduce stress in a short space of time. By focusing on positive emotions and engaging in activities that promote happiness, we can cultivate a more positive outlook and improve our overall quality of life.

TOOL 4

How to Power Stretch – give me just one minute!

You can do this at sitting or standing.

If you are sitting, think of your posture, with your bottom at the back of the chair, feet hip-width apart, your head, neck and shoulders and back relaxed, and looking forwards.

If you're standing, stand with good posture, with a natural curve of your spine, your feet hip-width apart and a slight bend in your knees, and looking forwards.

First, place your hands on your hips.

Then place your hands at the side of your neck; do not poke your head forwards. Gently squeeze your elbows back until you feel a gentle or good stretch in your chest and shoulders; this also strengthens your mid back muscles.

Raise your arms in the air above you, wherever is comfortable for you, and then bring your arms back down and place your hands back on your hips again.

You can breathe naturally, or you can add some breathing into the exercise by following the instruction below.

Breathe in through your nose. As you breathe out through your mouth, place your hands at the side of your neck and squeeze your elbows back until you feel a gentle stretch in your chest and shoulders.

As you move your arms up in the air, breathe in through the nose. As you exhale, float your arms back down, placing your hands back on your hips.

Repeat – 5 times or for one minute.

This exercise will help to improve posture and release muscles, stretching your chest and shoulders, strengthening mid back, and helping you to feel more confident, happier and more powerful.

Check in with yourself. How do you feel now?

Try it out before a stressful meeting or on arrival at work.

CHAPTER FIVE

STRESS TO CALM WITH HAPPINESS

Tip: Remember it's just ONE minute – and you can CHOOSE happiness!

What's the lowdown?

The concept of choosing happiness involves recognising happiness as a choice that we can make in any moment, regardless of external circumstances. By changing our thoughts and focusing on positive emotions, we can move from feeling stressed to calm in a very short space of time. Posture can also play a role in this process, as adopting a more upright and confident posture can help to improve mood and reduce stress.

Studies have shown that choosing happiness and changing our state can have a range of benefits. One study published in *The Journal of Positive Psychology* found that simply recalling a positive memory for one minute can lead to significant increases in positive emotions and decreases in negative emotions. Another study published in the journal *Emotion* found that adopting a more upright and open body posture can increase feelings of power and confidence, leading to more positive emotions.

Engaging in positive activities, such as expressing gratitude or performing acts of kindness, can also lead to improvements in psychological wellbeing and reductions in stress.

By taking back control over our unconscious mind and changing our body posture to feel happier, we can improve our wellbeing and reduce stress in a short space of time.

'I am in charge of how I feel and today I am choosing happiness.'
Maya Angelou, civil rights activist and author

One very simple way of 'choosing happiness' is to consciously smile. This can be very powerful in reducing stress and improving your wellbeing.

In the film *Eat Pray Love*, taken from the book of the same name by Elizabeth Gilbert, you may remember the charming Medicine Man, who told Julia Roberts' character to smile. So smile! You can even try smiling – with your liver! We'll teach you how to do this in the Bonus Tool at the end of this chapter.

Smiling has a profound impact on our mental and physical health. Have you heard of the Facial Feedback Hypothesis? This suggests that the muscles involved in producing a smile can actually send signals to the brain, triggering the release of hormones and neurotransmitters associated with positive emotions. In other words, smiling can lead to the experience of happiness and wellbeing, even if it initially feels forced or inauthentic.

When we smile, our brain triggers a cascade of physiological responses that contribute to our overall wellbeing. Research has shown that the facial muscles involved in smiling send signals to the brain, stimulating the release of endorphins, dopamine and serotonin, which are the neurotransmitters associated with feelings of happiness, pleasure and relaxation. These natural 'feel-good' chemicals can counteract stress hormones such as cortisol, leading to a more tranquil state of mind.

Smiling not only influences our brain chemistry but also affects our body's stress response system. A study conducted by Kraft and Pressman (2012) revealed that even participants who were instructed to hold a 'forced' smile experienced a decrease in heart rate and a reduction in self-reported stress levels compared to a neutral facial expression. This suggests that the act of smiling can modulate our autonomic nervous system, promoting relaxation and calmness.

Amy Cuddy, a social psychologist and Harvard Business School professor, conducted a notable study on the power of smiling and its impact on stress reduction. In her research, Cuddy and her colleagues explored the concept of *fake it till you make it* by investigating whether the physical act of smiling, even if induced artificially, could influence an individual's stress response. The study involved participants holding a pencil between their teeth, to create a smile-like expression, while performing stressful tasks. The results of Cuddy's study were remarkable. Participants who maintained a forced smile, even with the pencil between their teeth, showed decreased stress levels compared to those who maintained a neutral facial expression. These findings suggest that the physical act of smiling, regardless of its authenticity, can have a genuine impact on reducing stress and promoting wellbeing.

Interestingly, the benefits of smiling extend beyond our individual experience. When we smile, we activate mirror neurons, which are specialised cells in our brain that mimic the facial expressions of others. These mirror neurons can trigger a positive feedback loop by prompting others to smile back, leading to a contagious effect of happiness and stress reduction. When we smile, and others smile back, we create a supportive environment.

So, the evidence is clear: smiling has the power to reduce stress and promote wellbeing. Even if it feels forced at first, the act of smiling can help create a positive feedback loop, leading to genuine feelings of happiness and wellbeing.

For this exercise we have combined smiling, breathing, a positive affirmation and a power pose so we get 4 for the price of 1 as it were!

TOOL 5

The Happy Exercise – give me just one minute!

Sitting or standing with good posture, close your eyes, relax your arms by your side and take 5 relaxing breaths in and out.

Breathe in through your nose and exhale through your mouth. Remember to relax.

Do this 5 times, slowly and with intention.

Then to energise and to bring more happiness, confidence and success – *SMILE!* Smile big. Smile wide!

Open your eyes, place your hands in a fist by your shoulders or wherever is comfortable and then punch your arms upwards high in the air 10 times saying the positive affirmation **'well done'**. (You can say this silently or out loud.)

Well done, well done, well done, well done, well done!

(Keep smiling as you punch the arms in the air.)

Well done, well done, well done, well done, well done!

Repeat this exercise anytime you are stressed, at the desk, at home or even when you're out and about. OK, so you might get some looks if the office is busy, or you start punching the air on the train, but as always ... adapt to suit! Remember that just visualising you are punching the air is effective too!

At regular intervals during the day, when you become conscious of it, break into a smile, however daft it feels. Remember studies, really have proven the power of the physiology of a smile.

Bonus Tool

If you want to choose to smile with different parts of your body – such as your liver – try this.

Breathe in and out and take notice of your flow or breath as you pay attention in your mind to your liver, which is near the bottom of your ribcage to the right, or to whichever part of your body you are imagining. Then notice how you feels as you imagine it smiling.

CHAPTER SIX

STRESS TO CALM AND THE POWER OF JOURNALING

Tip: Remember it's just ONE minute –
and it's ONLY read by you!

What's the lowdown?

The act of writing down our thoughts, feelings and aspirations has been shown to have numerous benefits for our mental, emotional and even physical wellbeing in recent years. It's a simple yet profound practice that can allow us to let our thoughts flow and potentially unearth some thoughts and emotions that would otherwise remain hidden.

Journaling is the act of expressing our innermost thoughts and emotions through the written word. It provides a safe and private space for us to explore our desires, fears and dreams – without judgment or interruption. By putting pen to paper, we create a tangible reflection of our inner landscape, allowing us to gain clarity, discover patterns and unearth hidden treasures within ourselves. Notice we said, 'pen to paper', because it's definitely advantageous to write the old-fashioned way, by hand, rather than using a keyboard, because it's better for the cognitive brain.

Julia Cameron, a highly acclaimed author and creativity expert, has inspired millions of people to tap into their creative potential through her international bestselling book *The Artist's Way*. She introduces the practice of Morning Pages, a form of journaling where we are encouraged to write three pages of stream-of-consciousness thoughts each morning. Doing this daily makes it almost like a ritual, or a form of meditation, and it helps us to clear our mind, release self-doubt and negative talk onto the page (better out than in!) and even start to feel creative.

'Doing something that is productive is a great way to alleviate emotional stress. Get your mind doing something that is productive.'

Ziggy Marley, musician

Writing our thoughts down without judgement, or editing, can help to alleviate stress and foster self-empowerment through positive affirmations. When we write about our worries, anxieties and frustrations, we externalise them, giving them less power over us. The mere act of acknowledging and articulating our stressors can bring a sense of relief and create space for problem-solving.

As Louise Hay, founder of Hay House Publishing, said, 'You can't clean the house till you can see the dirt.' If we are keeping it all hidden, it will be harder to deal with.

Journaling allows us to counteract negative self-talk by replacing it with positive affirmations. By intentionally affirming our worth, strengths and aspirations, we can cultivate a mindset of self-compassion and resilience.

There is scientific evidence on the impact of journaling on wellbeing. A study conducted by Dr James W. Pennebaker, a leading researcher in the field of expressive writing, provides compelling evidence for the benefits of journaling. In his research, Dr Pennebaker found that individuals who engaged in expressive writing about their deepest emotions experienced significant improvements in their overall wellbeing. This included reductions in stress, improved immune function and enhanced psychological resilience. The study's findings highlight the transformative power of journaling as a therapeutic tool for personal growth and emotional healing.

So, grab a pen and a blank page and embark on the remarkable adventure of journaling. Your inner world and your inner power await!

TOOL 6

Grab a Pen and Journal – give me just one minute!

Here is a simple way of journaling while you are at your desk, or on the train, for one minute with positive affirmations.

1. Get a notebook or piece of paper – or maybe treat yourself to a special journal.

2. Pick a positive affirmation and write it down – there's a list below to help you get started.

3. Write about what the message means to you. Don't think too hard about this, write whatever comes into your mind straight away.

Keep an eye on the time so you spend only one minute – set a timer if needed.

You may find you jot down some rather random things, which is fine. You may come up with action steps or ideas, or it may encourage you to explore other things.

Write freely. Think about your body and your posture when writing and try to sit with good posture. You could even try the SMILE tool!

Positive affirmations to choose from – or you can use one of your own.

I am loved, I am surrounded by love.

When negativity appears, I find a solution, talk to those I trust and think positively.

I love to smile; smiling makes me happy.

I am creative.

I am energetic.

I am healthy.

I have good relationships.

It's OK to be me.

I love setting goals.

I am peaceful.

I take breaks and rest to recharge my batteries.

I sleep well.

I am patient.

I breathe and relax.

I am calm.

I am enthusiastic.

I am OK with asking for help.

I am solution focused.

A Bonus Tool

You can extend this exercise by closing your eyes and visualising your goals or action steps that you are going to take; daydream about it. Afterwards, write down what came to you.

This exercise is another form of meditation and can be helpful in guiding you with decision making and planning in work and life in general.

If you enjoy journaling and would like to spend longer on this exercise, go for it! You could find this becomes a wonderful new regular practice.

CHAPTER SEVEN

STRESS TO CALM WITH SETTING GOALS AND VISUALISATION

Tip: Remember it's just ONE minute –
and you can ACHIEVE your goals!

What's the lowdown?

Setting goals can be incredibly beneficial for both our work and personal lives. It gives us something to strive towards and helps us to focus our energy and efforts. Goals also give us a sense of purpose and motivation, and they can provide a framework for making decisions and prioritising tasks. We can't tell you what goals to set, but we *can* help you achieve them.

Research has shown that setting goals can be a powerful tool for personal and professional development. A study published in the *Journal of Applied Psychology* found that individuals who set specific, challenging goals performed better than those who set vague or easy goals.

Additionally, the study found that setting goals was associated with higher levels of motivation and job satisfaction (Locke and Latham, 2002).

'I am stronger than my challenges, and my challenges are making me stronger.'
Karen Salmansohn, behavioural change expert

Visualising the achievement of our goals can also have a powerful impact. This technique has been used by athletes and performers for decades to help them achieve their goals. By visualising ourselves successfully achieving our goals, we can create a mental blueprint that helps us to stay focused and motivated.

In the workplace most of us are aware of the **SMART** model to set effective goals: **S**pecific, **M**easurable, **A**chievable, **R**elevant and **T**ime-bound. Let's work with this model.

We need to start by thinking about what we want to achieve, our goal. Then break it down into smaller, manageable steps. Write it down, make it measurable within these steps, ensure it is achievable and realistic, and that it is relevant to what you want to achieve. Then put together a schedule of time in which you hope to achieve your goals. It's important to review this regularly to ensure you stay on track.

Incorporating visualisation into the goal-setting process is a way of focusing on how it will feel when you have accomplished what you have set out to do, and it is a great way of keeping motivated and focused.

We know that setting goals works, but when we incorporate visualisation it's especially powerful.

Feeling positive when we visualise our goals is important too. If we engage with positive self-affirmations, it can lead us to more optimism, greater happiness in our challenges and see less anger and less stress in the whole process.

TOOL 7

Reaching Your Goals and Seeing the Success – give me just ONE minute!

Sitting or lying down, close your eyes. You can even do this at your desk. Close your eyes and breathe and relax, breathing into your nose and out through your mouth.

Give yourself permission to think of a goal. This can be small or big – the ultimate big goal or part of the smaller steps to help achieve this. Choose something that is personal for you.

Breathe in and out slowly and relax both your body and your mind.

Give yourself permission to see your goal, to hear what it sounds like, to feel it, to know something about it. Then breathe and relax, saying to yourself silently, *thank you for [this goal]*, being explicit about what your goal is. Say thank you as if the goal has already been achieved. Enjoy this feeling of reaching your goal, this feeling of success.

Take a minute to do this and then open your eyes. Write down your chosen goal for this exercise and any insights that came to you during this time of visualising your goal and its success. These insights can be useful in helping you put small steps in place to make your visualisation a reality.

Are there any action steps that you need to take now to help you reach your goal?

CONCLUSION

CALM ...

We really hope that you have enjoyed this book and have made the decision to try some or all the tools in your everyday life. We hope you are feeling calm.

'Calmness is the cradle of power.'
Josiah Gilbert Holland, author

Remember that reducing stress and anxiety in our lives is paramount to achieving good health and a fulfilling life.

Remember that reducing long-term stress can have a positive effect on our physical, mental and emotional health, and help us to prevent chronic illness and other health issues.

By incorporating simple stress-reducing tools into our daily routines, we can significantly improve our wellbeing and overall sense of calm and balance.

From breathing techniques, mindfulness practices, positive affirmations, stretching and goal setting, we have explored simple tools that can be easily incorporated into even the busiest of schedules. No excuses, not even for busy lawyers!

These tools have been shown to have proven scientific benefits in reducing stress and anxiety, leading to improved overall health and happiness.

It is crucial to remind ourselves that taking care of our mental and emotional health is just as important as taking care of our physical health. By prioritising stress-reducing activities, we can lead a more balanced and fulfilling life, both at work and at home.

Remember, it's not what we do as a one-off that makes the difference; it's what becomes our daily 'self-care' practice. We urge you to implement these simple tools consistently and to achieve a healthier and happier life.

Remember, taking care of ourselves is a lifelong journey, and we owe it to ourselves to make our wellbeing a top priority. Self-care is *not* selfish, it's 'showing up' to be the best you can be.

Remember to say: **Just give me ONE minute!** That one minute of time can make all the difference to your day.

We welcome feedback as to how these tools have worked for you, so please don't hesitate to get in contact. We are here for you.

Beverley and Janey

X

Here are some tips that help us when we are stressed.

Tips from Janey

If I am really feeling anxious, and am at home, I put on a piece of music (usually something I loved as a teenager) and shake it out, literally dancing wildly (in private!!). It sorts everything out!

I remember the power of feeling grounded, taking off socks and shoes and going and standing on grass or the sand. If there is a tree nearby, I stop short of hugging it, but I do stand with my back against it and breathe.

If I am lucky enough to be by the sea, I walk by the waves. If not, I find a recording of waves and just listen, it calms me down.

Tips from Beverley

I'm not a morning person but having a hot shower and then a 30-second cold shower wakes me up, boosts my energy and puts me in a great mood.

If things get on top of me, I go for a walk, even just round the block, enjoying the cool crisp air and the quietness, listening (where possible) to the birds singing. It certainly helps to blow the cobwebs away.

I schedule a date with myself, time on my own to cycle or walk somewhere in nature, a park or by the sea. I take my journal with me and stop and write when I find a quiet bench, a quirky café for a coffee and cake or anywhere with beautiful scenery. I gift myself an hour, or two, to take time to relax.

Tips from lawyers for de-stressing at work

I take a break by getting up from my desk and doing something different – making a cup of tea, for example.

I find talking to colleagues helpful. We all go through similar things, and they sometimes understand.

Making sure I take a proper lunch break and going for a walk outside – anything to get out of the office for even five minutes helps.

Stretches and breathing exercises – they do work!

Tips from lawyers for de-stressing outside work

Taking part in exercise of any sort.

Talking to my partner and my family – they're very supportive.

Making time for hobbies, such as playing the piano or reading.

A change of scene – using the weekend for a day out or a mini holiday.

ABOUT THE AUTHORS

Beverley Densham, author of a number of books to include ***I Talk to Angels***, is an inspirational speaker and Mindfulness Pilates teacher and runs workshops and classes with her company Mindfulness Pilates. She works within law practices to promote the health and wellbeing of employees/lawyers. She regularly contributes articles to holistic and lifestyle magazines. She has a degree in Sports Science from University of Brighton.

www.beverleydensham.com

Linkedin @Beverley-densham

Instagram Beverley_densham

Twitter @BeverleyDensham

YouTube @mindfulnesspilates6603

Janey Lee Grace is an author and speaker. A former co-presenter on BBC Radio 2's *Steve Wright in the Afternoon* for 24 years, she was also a backing singer with Wham!, Kim Wilde and Boy George and had her own Number 8 chart hit as Cola Boy with '7 Ways to Love'. Janey has now written five books on holistic living, including the Number 1 Amazon bestseller ***Imperfectly Natural Woman***. Her latest book is ***Happy Healthy Sober***, which encourages everyone to look again at their relationship with alcohol.

www.janeyleegrace.com www.thesoberclub.com

Linkedin @janeyleegrace

Instagram @janeyleegrace

Twitter @janeyleegrace

REFERENCES AND FURTHER READING

1. Stress to Calm with Meditation

Creswell, J. D., Pacilio, L. E., Lindsay, E. K., and Brown, K. W., 'Brief mindfulness meditation training alters psychological and neuroendocrine responses to social evaluative stress', P*sychoneuroendocrinology*, 44, (2014), pp 1–12.

Epel, E. S., *et al*, 'Meditation and cortisol responses to stress: A randomized controlled trial', *Psychoneuroendocrinology* 68, (2016), pp 110–117.

Jerath, R., Edry, J. W., Barnes, V. A., and Jerath, V., 'Physiology of long pranayamic breathing: neural respiratory elements may provide a mechanism that explains how slow deep breathing shifts the autonomic nervous system', *Medical Hypotheses*, 67(3), (2006), pp 566–571.

Khoury, B., Sharma, M., Rush, S. E., and Fournier, C., 'Mindfulness-based stress reduction for healthy individuals: A meta-analysis', Journal of Psychosomatic Research, 78(6), (2015), pp 519–528.

Winfrey, O., 'The transformative power of meditation.' Oprah.com, (2013).

2. Stress to Calm with Positive Affirmations

Cascio, C. N. *et al.*, 'Self-affirmation activates brain systems associated with self-related processing and reward and is reinforced by future orientation', *Social Cognitive and Affective Neuroscience*, 11(4), (2016), pp 621–629.

Latham, G. P., and Locke, E. A., 'New Developments in and Directions for Goal-Setting Research', *European Psychologist*, 12(4), (2007), pp 290–300. https://doi.org/10.1027/1016-9040.12.4.290

Moser, J. S., Huppert, J. D., Duval, E., and Simons, R. F., 'Self-affirmation reduces cardiovascular reactivity to acute stress: Evidence from a real-world manipulation', *Journal of Health Psychology*, 35(9), (2016), pp 935–943

3. Stress to Calm with Neck and Shoulder Stretches

Jerath, R., Edry, J. W., Barnes, V. A., and Jerath, V., 'Physiology of long pranayamic breathing: neural respiratory elements may provide a mechanism that explains how slow deep breathing shifts the autonomic nervous system', *Medical Hypotheses*, 67(3), (2006), pp 566–571.

Pal, G. K., Velkumary, S., and Madanmohan, 'Effect of short-term practice of breathing exercises on autonomic functions in normal human volunteers', *Indian Journal of Medical Research*, 120(2), (2004), pp 115–121.

Telles, S., Singh, N., and Balkrishna, A., 'Heart rate variability changes during high frequency yoga breathing and breath awareness', *BioPsychoSocial Medicine*, 6(1), (2012), pp 1–7.

Zaccaro, A., *et al.*, 'How Breath-Control Can Change Your Life: A Systematic Review on Psycho-Physiological Correlates of Slow Breathing', *Frontiers in Human Neuroscience*, 12, (2018), p 353.

Zeidan, F., Johnson, S. K., Diamond, B. J., David, Z., and Goolkasian, P., 'Mindfulness meditation improves cognition: evidence of brief mental training', *Consciousness and Cognition*, 19(2), (2010), pp 597–605.

4. Stress to Calm with the Power stretch

Cuddy, A. J. 'Your body language may shape who you are', TED Talk, (2012). Retrieved from: https://youtu.be/Ks-_Mh1QhMc

Fredrickson, B. L., 'The Role of Positive Emotions in Positive Psychology: The Broaden-and-Build Theory of Positive Emotions', *American Psychologist*, 56(3), (2001), pp 218–226.

Fredrickson, B. L., Cohn, M. A., Coffey, K. A., Pek, J., and Finkel, S. M., 'Open hearts build lives: Positive emotions, induced through loving-kindness meditation, build consequential personal resources', *Journal of Personality and Social Psychology*, 95(5), (2008), pp 1045–1062.

Kruis, A., Tscharaktschiew, N., and Blanchard, C., 'Body posture effects on self-evaluation: A self-validation approach', *Emotion*, 18(4), (2018), pp 635–641.

5. Stress to Calm with choosing to Feel Happy

Abel, E. M., and Kruger, M. L., 'Smile Intensity in Photographs Predicts Longevity', *Psychological Science*, 21(4), (2010), pp 542–544.

Keysers, C., and Gazzola, V., 'Expanding the mirror: vicarious activity for actions, emotions, and sensations', *Current Opinion in Neurobiology*, 19(6), (2009), pp 666–671.

Kraft, T. L., and Pressman, S. D.,'Grin and Bear It: The Influence of Manipulated Facial Expression on the Stress Response', *Psychological Science*, 23(11), (2012), pp 1372–1378.

Soussignan, R. (2002) 'Duchenne smile, emotional experience, and autonomic reactivity', *Emotion*, 2(1), (2002), pp 52–75

6. Stress to Calm and the Power of Journaling

Pennebaker, J.W., 'Expressive Writing in Psychological Science', *Perspectives on Psychological Science*, 13(2), (2018), pp 226–229.

7. Stress to Calm with Setting Goals and Visualisation

Locke, E. A., and Latham, G. P., 'Building a practically useful theory of goal setting and task motivation: A 35-year odyssey', *American Psychologist*, 57(9), (2002), pp 705–717.

www.ingramcontent.com/pod-product-compliance
Ingram Content Group UK Ltd.
Pitfield, Milton Keynes, MK11 3LW, UK
UKHW051916060225
454773UK00009B/74

9 780857 162526